Summer-Rayne: Warrior Princess!

Copyright © 2019 by Summer-Rayne Bradford. All rights reserved.

No rights claimed for public domain material, all rights reserved. No parts of this publication may be reproduced, stored in any retrieval system, or transmitted in any form or by any means, electronic, mechanical, recording, or otherwise, without the prior written permission of the author. Violations may be subject to civil or criminal penalties.

ISBN:
978-1-63308-480-3 (paperback)
978-1-63308-481-0 (ebook)

Interior and Cover Design by *R'tor John D. Maghuyop*

CHALFANT ECKERT
PUBLISHING

1028 S Bishop Avenue, Dept. 178
Rolla, MO 65401

Printed in United States of America

Summer-Rayne Warrior Princess!

Written by:
Summer-Rayne Bradford

Thank you

First and foremost, thank YOU! Thank you to each and every individual that reads this story. I hope it brings you joy, makes you smile and most importantly begins a conversation.

Thank you to all the nurses and staff at Sick Kids Hospital, Toronto and Princess Margaret, Toronto. Without each and everyone of you our daughter and lots of other children wouldn't have a quality of life upon diagnosis. From early morning calls to interactions in the hallways, Summer's Team was always there to help! Something we are forever grateful for.

A special thank you to Nurse Susan at Princess Margaret. You are an angel on earth. Without your kind words, your early morning talks and your reassurance every morning before treatment, I don't know if we would have been able to get through this. Every word spoken was taken to heart and we will take with us till the end of time.

Thank you to our friends and family who have stuck by our sides. Without the support of you, our community and everyone in between we would have been lost. They say it takes a village to raise a child. I can't think of a more fitting saying. We have people who were once strangers now family. People we can all lean on for a shoulder to cry on, for a pick-me-up or to laugh uncontrollably. You have made this journey easier and for that, we thank you.

Special acknowledgement of Dason and Summer's Nana, for she is experiencing a battle of her own but shall she never feel alone. She is watched over by a Warrior Princess rooting for her along the way.

Thank you to Michael Flatley and his team for reaching out to us. Unfortunately, our paths crossed due to a devastating diagnosis, but we are thankful that people like you allow families to share their story, their way and on their terms. You and your team are extraordinary people to capture a glimpse into the lives of these children who have gone to battle in life.

Lastly, we want to thank our children, Summer-Rayne and Dason.

Miss Summer-Rayne, you have shown us what it means to be strong. You have been the one who has smiled through all of this. Our little girl, your diagnosis isn't rare, it's uncommon. You are what is rare. Always remember that. Your beyond loved every minute of every day.

Our Son, precious Dason. I am thankful that you are a strong boy yet emotional. Never let anyone take that away from you. You and your sister have been best friends from the beginning. The bond you share is unbreakable. Always remember that although our lives change, people come and go, one thing's for sure. You are your sister's brother, her hero and most importantly our special boy.

This book isn't only for our family but for every family battling in their own way. Forever know your in our thoughts and prayers.

On a big, old cattle farm
This story is written
Where a little girl spends her days
Playing and feeding the chickens

Summer-Rayne is her name, and
Everyday she wears a dress
Despite her royal appearance,
She loves the mud, and making a mess!

She is a princess and a tomboy,
A perfect mix
Dressed to perfection
As she does four wheeler tricks

Summer wears pretty dresses
With jewels to match
And muddy rubber pink boots
So her shoes do not clash

Everything Summer does
She does to the max
Playing in the fields
She never holds back

Her boots may be pretty
Like a princess's pink
But Summer plays so hard,
Boy, do those boots stink!

Summer loves to jump off couches
She jumps through the air
She flies around with her baby dolls in her arms
And mud still in her hair

Summer lives life to the fullest
She truly has no fear
She has no filter and takes no nonsense
Summer makes that quite clear

But this fun-loving girl's story
Has taken a serious turn
Doctors found a "boo boo" on her brain,
DIPG - she would learn

This diagnosis is so bad,
There is no real cure
A fight so hard,
A battle Summer endures

Nothing can stop Summer
From having her fun
She gets back to playing
As soon as treatment is done

Summer finds the positive
In all that she beholds
But her days are not like
A regular four year old's

Summer gets MRIs,
"Photo shoots for her brain"
These pictures show the doctors
Where Summer feels the pain

She needs to go through
Days of radiation
But Summer is so brave and so strong
She's an excellent patient

Never shy to talk about
Her treatments if you ask
Especially if you mention
Her very cool "goalie mask"

A die-hard Maple Leaf fan
Summer always shows her support
She pretends her treatment
Is just like her favorite sport

There are few like Summer,
That is for sure
But through the fun,
We must find a cure

This incredible young girl
Should not have to suffer
While her diagnosis is tough,
Summer-Rayne is tougher

Summer is the missing puzzle piece
That completes her family's puzzle
Together they are with her
During her struggle

No other piece can fit
Just like her
It's Mommy, Daddy,
Brother, and Sister

Proceeds raised from this book will go to the following organizations:

Montreal Children's Hospital
www.thechildren.com

Books That Heal
www.booksthatheal.org

www.ingramcontent.com/pod-product-compliance
Lightning Source LLC
Chambersburg PA
CBHW042027150426
43198CB00002B/95